Sakhi

PREMARITAL GUIDE TO
RELATIONSHIPS AND PARENTING

VIDYA SHANKAR CHAKRAVARTHY

ink Scribe

ink

Sakhi

Copyright © 2024 Vidya Shankar Chakravarthy

Publisher: Inkscirbe Publishing Pvt Ltd

ISBN Number: 978-1-966421-00-9

Contents

Thank You 5

Foreword 7

Introduction 9

1. Legal Information 11

2. Social Aspects 17

3. Physical Preparation 25

4. Mentally Preparing to Run a
    Household 31

5. Financial Prudence 39

6. Emotional Readiness 41

7. Spiritual Ascension 43

8. Pregnancy, Delivery and Parenting 59

9. In Closing 87

Book Reviews 89

Thank You

The motivation for creating this document comes from my personal life journey, during which I felt completely unprepared for marriage and its long term implications.

In India, young adults often enter the marriage arena straight out of college as newly minted graduates. Most of them take on the lifetime commitment with little or no preparedness or awareness of their rights and responsibilities. The non-judgemental support of my family helped me identify gaps in my relationship approaches and gain clarity on what marriage or separation entails. I have tried to pay their goodwill forward with this document that I hope serves as a ready reckoner on marriage for young people.

This document would not have been possible without the contributions of a few like-minded individuals. I extend my deepest gratitude to:

Interns Sharanya Vemaraju and Mira Dhinoo for helping me collate the referenced content.

Imran Ali Namazi, a *web developer*, *writer* and social entrepreneur, for compiling and editing the content besides designing the cover pages.

Justice Chandhru Krishnaswamy, Retd Judge, for reviewing the content prior to publishing and offering his expert opinion.

And, to everyone who shared statistics, facts and opinions with me to ensure the compilation of this comprehensive guidebook.

Foreword

Vidya Shankar Chakravarthy has done a commendable job in bringing out "Sakhi - a premarital guide to relationships and parenting" for the use of youngsters of these days who are attempting to enter into a marital bond. She had claimed in her book that the Indian girls who have completed education enter the marriage arena hardly aware of their rights, responsibilities and holistic life preparations needed. Why the girls alone? Even the boys need a better understanding on these issues.

Due to increased urban migration and the joint family system slowly getting broken down, the families have become atomic units. They don't get advice and counselling from the near and dear anymore. Each marriage becomes an experiment. The arranged marriages apart, the love marriages being on the increase and the couple choosing places of work across the seas they need a matured understanding of the relationships and parenting. This book somewhat fills up the gap and will be a useful guide.

Due to the increased marital discords, and the lack of specialisation of the civil judges on matrimonial matters, the Parliament thought of enacting a new law and accordingly introduced the Family Courts Act, 1984 by which an umbrella court to deal with all problems of matrimonial discords. However, these courts are only located in metropolitan towns and those who reside outside the metropolis are to be contended with the old civil courts.

The avowed object of the Act was to provide "the establishment of Family Courts with a view to promote conciliation in, and secure speedy settlement of disputes relating to marriage and family affairs and for matters connected therewith". Even selecting persons for appointment of judges to Family Courts, Section 4(4)(a) mandates "every endeavour shall be made to ensure that persons committed to the need to protect and preserve the institution of marriage and to promote the welfare of children and qualified by reason of their experience and expertise to promote the settlement of disputes by conciliation and counselling are selected;" In practice these aspirations are never fulfilled.

Though the Act provides for mandatory counselling between the parties, the efficacy of such counselling is seen as remote. The ever-increasing filing of cases and overburdening the courts resulting in long delays has come in for severe criticism in the public sphere. In any event, the courts are only meant for solving the marital discords and the related problems arising therein.

However, they are not created for solving issues beyond the marital discords. There are still issues among the couples relating to childbirth, adoption, and abortion etc. These issues also require certain enlightenment and the book covers the areas beyond court dockets.

Even on the question of abortion, some of the enlightened countries are backtracking. The recent reversal of the judgement on abortion rights rendered 50 years ago in Roe Vs. Wade, 1973 by the Supreme Court of the United States of America in Dobbs Vs. Jackson, 2022 has sent shockwaves. The women are yet to gain recognition over their body. In any event, an elementary knowledge on issues of premarital relationships and parenting is a must. I am glad Vidya has done a good work and it will be a useful guide for the youth of our time.

23.9.2024 **Justice K Chandru**

Chennai Retd. Judge, Madras High Court

Introduction

Sakhi is designed to serve as a comprehensive handbook for young people looking to make decisions about marriage and family life. With this intent, the author has drawn from her own marital experiences to highlight every aspect of marriage or separation and annulment to ensure that young adults, particularly girls, are fully informed of their rights and responsibilities.

The handbook outlines legal, physical, emotional, financial, and spiritual preparations, besides offering insights on conscious conception and early parenting.

Sakhi, the book aims to foster a generation of thoughtful individuals, whether they choose to share their lives with a partner or remain single.

Legal Information

01

The legal age for marriage in order to prevent child marriage:

- The definition of Child under the Prohibition of Child Marriage Act, 2006
- Section 2(a): "child" means a person who, if a male, has not completed twenty-one years of age, and if a female, has not completed eighteen years of age;

1.1 Rights of a Wife in the Hindu Marriage Act [1]

Right to matrimonial home:

Even when the husband dies, a wife retains the legal right of a wife over the husband to dwell in the marital home. Even if the residence is not of the husband's but rather his parents' or a leased flat, she has a right to reside. In the event of a divorce, she can remain in the marital home until a suitable alternative is found for her or she can return to her parent's home. The Hindu Marriage Act (HMA), 1955, has no provision for a married lady to return to her parent's home. She has the legal right of a wife over the husband to remain if and when she so desires. One of the important legal rights of a wife over the husband is the right to a matrimonial home.

Right to property:

According to an amendment of 2005 to the Hindu Succession Act (HSA) 1956, a daughter, whether married or not, has identical rights to inherit her father's property as her brother. A woman has the same legal right as a wife

---

[1] *https://www.ezylegal.in/blogs/what-are-the-legal-rights-of-a-wife-over-the-husband*

over the husband as other heirs to inherit her husband's property. She can only inherit it if her spouse hasn't made a will or hasn't left her out of it. If a husband remarries without dissolving the former marriage, the first wife retains ownership of the property. One of the legal rights of a wife over the husband is to own the property of her husband.

Right to report domestic violence:

The Protection of Women Under Domestic Violence Act of 2005 allows a woman to report domestic violence. This law makes physical, mental, sexual, financial, and other types of abuse illegal. She is entitled to protection, support, custody, and compensation, as well as the right to remain in the same residence. One of the legal rights of a wife over the husband is the right to report domestic violence.

Right to abortion:

The Medical Termination of Pregnancy Act of 1971 offers a woman complete autonomy over whether or not to terminate a child without her husband's consent. The maximum time a kid can be aborted has been upped to 24 weeks. The right to abortion is one of the legal rights of a wife over the husband.

Right to divorce:

The Hindu Marriage Act of 1955 grants women the legal right of a wife over the husband to divorce without their husband's approval. Adultery, cruelty, desertion, eviction from the marital home, mental illness, and other reasons can be used to get a divorce. The act also allows for divorce by mutual consent. There are various additional grounds for the wife as a legal right of a wife over the husband.

Right to seek maintenance and alimony:

A married woman has the legal right of a wife over the husband to request lifelong maintenance from her husband under the provisions of the law. If a marriage fails, the Hindu Marriage Act gives women the legal right of a wife over husband to seek support for themselves and their children from their husbands both during (interim maintenance) and after divorce (permanent maintenance). The court determines the amount of maintenance, which excludes Stree Dhan, based on the husband's income and living situation (includes up to 25 percent of it). This is one of the most important legal rights of a wife over the husband.

Resource: Hindu Marriage Act of 1955

Dowry prohibition and harassment:

The Dowry Prohibition Act of 1961 makes the dowry system illegal. A lady can file a complaint against her parents or in-laws for a dowry exchange. Any dowry-related abuse she encounters from her in-laws is a punishable offence under the law. The law punishes cruelty, domestic violence (physical, emotional, or sexual harassment), abetment to suicide, and dowry death as forms of dowry harassment of the bride. Although marital rape is not yet illegal in India, forced sex is covered by the Domestic Violence Act and Dowry Harassment.

Right to marry without rituals:

Section 7A of the Hindu Marriage Act in Tamil Nadu by which self-respect marriages without any rituals are also accepted.

T.N. Registration of Marriages Act, 2009 by which all religious marriages should be compulsorily registered. This safeguards a woman protecting her marital status.

1.2   Christian Marriage Act

In India, Christian personal laws relating to marriages, divorce, and succession are primarily governed by the Indian Christian Marriage Act of 1872 and the Indian Succession Act, of 1925. They protect the rights of Christian marriages and inheritance.

- **Divorce** – The Act provides for the dissolution of Christian marriages through divorce. Grounds for divorce are outlined and procedures for obtaining a divorce are specified.
- **Matrimonial causes** – Matters related to the restitution of Conjugal Rights, Judicial Separation, and Nullity of marriage are covered under this Act.

- **International perspective** – Universal Declaration of Human Rights- The UDHR, adopted by the United Nations, outlines fundamental human rights, regardless of religion. Also includes principles of equality, dignity, and freedom from discrimination.
- **Religious freedom protections** – Many countries, influenced by international norms, have laws protecting religious freedom. These laws aim to ensure that individuals, including Christian women, can practise their faith without fear of discrimination or persecution.

Property and inheritance rights of women under Christian law –

1. **Property rights of wife and widow** – According to Christian law, if a wife does not receive maintenance from her husband, she can file for divorce from her husband. After her husband's death, a widow can inherit one-third of his property. Children get the remaining shares. She will receive half of her husband's property if there are no children. The Christian law caps the minimum amount to Rs. 5000 that a wife can inherit from her dead husband.

2. **Property rights of daughter** – A daughter in a Christian family shall get an equal share of her paternal properties apart from her siblings. She is eligible to reside on her paternal property and receive maintenance from her parents until she marries a man. After marriage, her husband is responsible for maintaining her requirements.

3. **Property rights of mother** – According to women's property rights in Christian law, a mother is not dependent on her children. Mother, a mother cannot get maintenance. However, if her child dies and has no children, then the mother is eligible to receive one-fourth of his property.

Appendix: Indian Christian Marriage Act, 1872. [2]

---

[2] *https://aishwaryasandeep.in/protection-of-womens-right-in-christianity/*

1.3 Muslim Marriage Act

- The Muslim Women (Protection of Rights on Marriage) Actl, 2019 was introduced in Lok Sabha by the Minister of Law and Justice, Mr. Ravi Shankar Prasad on June 21, 2019. It replaces an Ordinance promulgated on February 21, 2019.

- The Act makes all declarations of talaq, including in written or electronic form, to be void (i.e. not enforceable in law) and illegal. It defines talaq as talaq-e-biddat or any other similar form of talaq pronounced by a Muslim man resulting in instant and irrevocable divorce. Talaq-e-biddat refers to the practice under Muslim personal laws where pronouncement of the word 'talaq' thrice in one sitting by a Muslim man to his wife results in an instant and irrevocable divorce.

- **Offence and penalty**: The Act makes declaration of talaq a cognizable offence, attracting up to three years' imprisonment with a fine. (A cognizable offence is one for which a police officer may arrest an accused person without warrant.) The offence will be cognizable only if information relating to the offence is given by: (i) the married woman (against whom talaq has been declared), or (ii) any person related to her by blood or marriage.

- The Act provides that the Magistrate may grant bail to the accused. The bail may be granted only after hearing the woman (against whom talaq has been pronounced), and if the Magistrate is satisfied that there are reasonable grounds for granting bail.

- The offence may be compounded by the Magistrate upon the request of the woman (against whom talaq has been declared). Compounding refers to the procedure where the two sides agree to stop legal proceedings, and settle the dispute. The terms and conditions of the compounding of the offence will be determined by the Magistrate.

- **Allowance**: A Muslim woman against whom talaq has been declared, is entitled to seek subsistence allowance from her husband for herself and for her dependent children. The amount of the allowance will be determined by the Magistrate.

- **Custody**: A Muslim woman against whom such talaq has been declared, is entitled to seek custody of her minor children. The manner of custody will be determined by the Magistrate.

Appendix: *https://www.indiacode.nic.in/bitstream/ 123456789/11564/1/a2019-20.pdf*

1.4　Special Marriage Act

The Special Marriage Act 1954 allows people to marry without considering their religion or caste. It promotes unity, equality, and individual rights to create social harmony and inclusivity. This law protects and recognises couples' love. The Special Marriage Act is important in India. This Act allows people to choose their partners and promotes a harmonious society.

Appendix: Special_Marriage_Act_1954.pdf

1.5　Other acts that refer to a married woman's rights

Appendix: Laws related to women.docx

1.6　Overseas living and access to marital support services

Appendix: TheForeignMarriageAct1969.pdf

Appendix: marriages-to-overseas-indians-booklet.pdf

Conclusion

Readers may further wish to read the book "Listen to my Case"[3] by Justice K Chandru.

---

[3] *amazon.in/Listen-Women-Approach-Courts-Tamil/dp/8194475937*

Social Aspects

wespath.com[4] advises the following tips for a healthy marriage.

1. Spend time with each other
2. Learn to negotiate conflict
3. Show respect for each other at all times
4. Learn about yourself first
5. Explore intimacy
6. Explore common interests
7. Create a spiritual connection
8. Improve your communication skills
9. Forgive each other
10. Look for the best in each other

2.1 Prevalent norms and expectations of married women

Indian society is diverse in nature. Like many other nations, India has a history of a patriarchal society where the primary power has been traditionally concentrated in the hands of men. Patriarchy refers to a social system where men hold the dominant role in political leadership, social privilege and economic power.

In India, there are certain prevalent norms and expectations of married women. This may vary between the urban and rural areas and between classes and castes.

---

[4] *wespath.org/health-well-being/health-well-being-resources/social-well-being/10-tips-for-a-healthy-marriage*

What is it that the husbands expect from their wives?

Husbands expect their wife to become a companion, she is expected to give love and affection to him unconditionally regardless of the wrongs and harm done to her. He expects support, validation, recognition and cooperation.

Some norms and expectations of married women in the Indian society are:

1. **Arranged marriage**: In many parts of India, arranged marriages are still a norm. Here more than a person selecting their own life partner, their families play a more significant role in selecting the spouse.

2. **Homemaker**: Married women in India are expected to take on the role of homemaker, manage the household, cook, clean, bear and take care of children, adhering to what her spouse and in-laws expect from her.

3. **Modesty**: While men are allowed to dress and behave as they wish, women are often expected to dress modestly, behave poised and conservatively.

4. **Early years**: A man of whichever age prefers to have a wife who is younger. Women who surpass the age of 30 find it hard to be seen as a suitable match for a man of any age.

5. **Joint family system**: Most prevalent in India, in a joint family system the woman when married is expected to move in with her husband and her in-laws under one roof. She is expected to show respect and deference to her husband's parents and extended family members. She is required to not only take care of herself and her husbands but also her in-laws and other family members.

6. **Cultural and religious practices**: Women are expected to participate in and uphold all cultural and religious practices, including fasting, attending ceremonies and observing rituals associated with her husband's family.

7. **Domestic violence and gender based discrimination**: Unfortunately, women across the globe face domestic violence and gender based discriminations. They are manipulated into thinking that it is normal behaviour, while it is purely wrong. This restricts them from speaking up about their experiences and seeking justice.

2.2 Where to draw the line

betterlyf.com makes these observations[5]

To set boundaries, women need to communicate and voice out their needs. So, what are the boundaries?

- Being aware of your needs.
- Being aware of what hurts you.
- Being aware of what you like and prefer.
- Learning to distinguish between what is acceptable and what is not.
- And clearly stating them out.
- Because it is an external expression of our internal self-affirmation.

Signs your boundaries are getting violated

- Are you feeling emotionally/mentally exhausted?
- Are you feeling dissatisfied?
- Are you a giver in your relationship?
- Are you able to manage your time?
- Are you able to achieve goals?

And in another article, goodmenproject.com states[6]

- When should you set boundaries?
- Keep them clear
- Don't let others cross the line
- Some boundaries to consider

---

[5] *betterlyf.com/articles/stress-and-anxiety/where-to-draw-the-line-in-relationships/*
[6] *goodmenproject.com/featured-content/when-to-draw-the-line-in-marriage-bh/*

2.3   Responsibility towards extended families

theconversation.com says the secret is in flexible roles[7].

Both men and women have equal responsibility for domestic and caretaker tasks within the family, on the basis of fair agreement and commitment. Doing the dishes, laundry, ironing, cooking, feeding the baby and so on are not solely the wife's job, but also the responsibility of the husband. Equal doesn't mean similar. So different families might apportion tasks in different ways to each member of the family.

The second idea is that both men and women have equal responsibilities to earn money and to participate actively within the community.

2.4   Developing a community of friends

marriage.com says about friendships that[8]

Couples are often faced with tension when it comes to friendships outside of their relationship. Conflict can arise when one person has the need to be social and included with others and the other desires alone time and is withdrawn from social events.

Friendships provide support, keep us from feeling lonely, and make us well-rounded people. Encouraging and supportive friends understand that your best-friend is, and should be, your spouse, but no matter how close we are to our spouse and kids, we often desire to have a kinship with others. Here are a few tips

- Balance
- Priorities
- How to maintain friendships
- Set boundaries
- Make time
- Give and take
- Make new friends

---

[7] *theconversation.com/the-secret-to-a-happy-marriage-flexible-roles-101275*
[8] *marriage.com/advice/relationship/friendships-after-marriage/*

Community of Friends

Friendships where there is no judgement or guilt tripping are certainly assets for any human being and most essentially a part of a married couple's lives. In the absence of elders who we may think of as outdated in their perceptions, nonjudgmental friendships become our sounding board for relaying anxieties or challenges. Satsang or meeting of friends regularly helps sustain energies to reinvest into a relationship.

2.5   Dignity

This pdf resource from learningpartnership.org[9] says that

Human dignity is valued in all cultures, yet its hard to pinpoint what it exactly connotes. Frequently we understand the parameters of human dignity only when they get eroded.

Jack Donnelly argues that human rights are a precondition for human dignity, while Diane Ayton-Shenker argues that the common value of human dignity is the foundation for human rights. The Preamble to the Universal Declaration of Human Rights (UDHR) suggests that human rights and human dignity are indivisible.

There is an increased need to emphasise the common, core values shared by all cultures: the value of life, social order and protection from arbitrary rule. These basic values are embodied in human rights. Traditional cultures should be approached and recognized as partners to promote greater respect for and observance of human rights.

2.6   Security

psychcentral.com talks of safety and security thus[10]

A healthy marriage is one in which both members of the couple feel safe. It is only when there is a foundation of safety that the individuals

---

[9] *https://learningpartnership.org/sites/default/files/resources/pdfs/ Session%20 2%20Human%20Dignity%2C%20Physical%20Integrity%2C%20and%20the%20 Rights%20of%20Husbands%20and%20Wives.pdf*
[10] *psychcentral.com/lib/a-good-marriage-is-a-safe-marriage*

as well as the couple can grow and mature. With it comes the intimacy that is only possible when people feel secure enough to be vulnerable. Without it, any conflict threatens the entire relationship.

[Often, couples] come for counselling because they long for the connection they once had or their efforts at connection aren't working. "We can't communicate" really means "we're not connecting." Often enough, one or the other (or both) doesn't feel safe enough to be 100 percent in the relationship.

A good marriage is one in which each partner consistently works on the following elements of safety:

- Security
- Trust
- Honesty
- Mutual respect
- Fidelity
- Platinum rule
- Emotional availability
- Clean fighting

Marriages that last are built on safety. Without it, neither member of the couple can relax into the relationship. With it, each person becomes a better version of themselves and the marriage grows in strength and intimacy.

And covenantkeepers.org says[11]

If you sense this lack of security in your relationship, is there a way it can be restored? Do you have to continue living with uncertainty and the anxiety of questioning your mate's love? Is there a solution to this doubt and insecurity? I believe there is an answer to this dilemma.

What is it like living with insecurity in your marriage?

---

[11] *covenantkeepers.org/online-articles/47-general-marital-issues/ 343-building-security-in-your-marriage*

How do you build security with your spouse?

1. Where is real security found?
2. Deal with your feelings.
3. Confront the issues head-on.
4. Love does not force.
5. Stop stumbling behaviour.
6. Choose to love.
7. Be balanced.
8. Focus on communication.
9. Become better friends.
10. Give them their freedom.

2.7 Compatibility

What does being compatible mean? Being *compatible means* the ability to co-exist or live together in unity and harmony without any disagreement. Some of the following terms qualify as compatible, agreeable, adaptable, cooperative, appropriate, attuned, corresponding, etc.

According to psychologist Mert Seker, adaptation is vital for healthy relationships.

- **Physical attraction**: The earliest sign of compatibility is the presence of being physically attracted to your partner, this sets the foundation to most relationships.
- **Common goals and interests**: Having common interests and goals make a compatible couple. Not all interests need to be shared but it is obvious that you would not be compatible in your relationships if your interests and goals don't align.
- **Willingness to grow together**: Most successful relationships result from both partners' willingness to grow together morally and learn and overcome their mistakes.
- **Patience**: To grow together, you must be patient with your partner. Impatience is a sign of incompatibility.

- **Similar philosophies**: Couples are compatible if they see the world through similar lenses. It need not be the exact same but some sort of a middle ground must exist.
- **Blame**: Playing the blame game is very easy but can instantly ruin a relationship. If you or your partner are always blaming you for your relationship not working it is evident that the relationship is not compatible.
- **Priority**: Both partners in a relationship must prioritise each other, their desires and the relationship. If this is not the case it can lead to a lot of tension and problems.

The bottom line is that compatibility is key for a successful relationship. It is important for couples to check their compatibility before entering into marriage or a relationship.

huffpost.com says[12]

look at these eight factors for compatibility.

1. Conversation
2. Intimacy
3. Relaxation
4. Ambition
5. Philosophy
6. Interests
7. Respect
8. Passion

---

[12] *huffpost.com/entry/8-elements-of-compatibili_b_5670285*

Physical Preparation

03

Physical preparation before marriage is a personal choice and can vary greatly depending on an individual and their health, fitness goals and preferences. Physical preparation is a very common aspect of preparation for marriage for both men and women. Before one gets married they must focus not only on their financial and mental well-being but their physical well-being as well. [13] [14] [15]

1. Regular exercise: Engaging in regular physical exercise is essential for both mental and physical well-being. This helps reduce stress, improve one's mood, improve lifestyle and boost confidence. One can choose between doing yoga, cardio or strength training etc.

2. Balanced diet: One must not just physically engage in activity but also maintain a balanced and well nutritious diet, this is a crucial aspect of ensuring one stays healthy and immune to illness. One must ensure to be consuming the right foods and every meal according to their health and health restrictions, this can be done with the help of a dietician.

3. Hydration: staying hydrated is essential for good health, now when we look for the solution of almost every illness it has something to do with consumption of water or variations of infused water. Drinking adequate amounts of water and liquids throughout the day keeps our body and minds functioning well.

---

[13] *https://www.brides.com/story/things-every-woman-should-do-before-getting-married*
[14] *https://www.heronridgeassocs.com/questions-before-marriage/*
[15] *https://azislam.com/how-to-prepare-yourself-for-marriage-in-islam*

4. Regular check-ups: before one thinks they should get married they should get checked for any illness or disease, this can help in transparency in the marriage making communication better which enhances the marriage.

5. Fertility and family planning: if one plans on getting married, they must be open to having difficult conversations on if they would like to start a family or not, addressing fertility concerns and consulting a healthcare professional if necessary.

3.1 Commitment to health and wellbeing[16]

Role-of-Good-Sleep-in-Everyday-life-(13-July-2021)—.pdf

Commitment to health and well- being is an important aspect in life itself, not just as a pre wedding preparation. It is necessary for a fulfilling and balanced life involving conscious and consistent choices to prioritise one's mental, physical, emotional health. Some key elements of commitment to health and well-being are:

1. Goal setting: to begin with committing to a healthy lifestyle, one must set goals for themselves, having goals set makes things clear and motivates one to fulfil them.

2. Healthy habits: establish and maintain healthy habits, like maintaining a routine, proper hygiene, a balanced diet etc.

3. Regular physical activity: engaging in regular physical activity is essential for physical well being and elevating one's mood. Finding what works for you and incorporating it into your daily routine is essential for maintaining physical health.

4. Adequate sleep: sleep is an essential part of one's routine. No matter the stream of profession one is in, they must ensure to maintain 7-9 hours of sleep per night for one's well being so they can function well through the day. This helps one's mental health, with managing stress as well as for physical well-being

---

[16] *https://www.ncbi.nlm.nih.gov/pmc/articles/PMC4275835/*

5. Regular check-ups: one must not skip routine check-ups and screenings. This helps a person identify and address health issues before it is too late.

6. Social life: maintaining a routine and being physically active is important but maintaining strong beneficial social connections with family and friends helps one not feel lonely. Cultivating positive relationships helps us when we are facing challenges.

3.2 Health and nutrition one needs to know about

THAC publication and exec summary of Fit for Life

Further Reading: FIT FOR LIFE[17]

Health and nutrition are both closely interrelated, having a good understanding of both is essential for maintaining a healthy lifestyle. Depending on who you ask, everyone seems to have different tips, tricks and advice regarding health and nutrition.

Healthy eating matters, food is what fuels us and delivers the calories that our bodies need to function well. If one's diet is deficit in calories or more, your health will suffer. This can risk illness in the heart, liver and can cause diabetes. Foods which are ultra processed can cause greater health conditions like cancer.

NUTRIENTS

Certain people stick to certain diets, but there is not one singular healthy diet that is universal, it always depends on the person, the circumstances, their financial state and their health.

Even though calories are important, it is the nutrients that matter. All foods contain calories, but not all calories contain nutrients.

---

[17] *https://pdfcoffee.com/fit-for-life-pdf-free.html*

DIET

Diet diversity is important, maintaining a healthy lifestyle need not be a boring one. They should find ways to incorporate what they love into their diet without it being harmful. Eating a balanced nutritious diet is very important and incorporating new nutritious foods can be a problem If you are a picky eater but it is still a necessity.

HIGH PROCESSED FOODS

One need not altogether avoid processed foods as that is not possible as even canned vegetables are processed. The best way to improve one's diet is to cut back on highly processed foods and ultra processed foods which can cause depression, obesity and heart problems.

TIPS

One must come to terms with their own body and mind to be able to have a healthy relationship with food. They must identify their allergies and what they lack and try to incorporate it into their diets. One must try and cut down on excess oils and sugars as well as processed items, they can do this by

1. Cooking at home
2. Honouring their dislikes into their diet
3. Choosing filling foods which are healthy
4. Cutting down on sugar
5. Eating whole foods
6. Hydrating but not over-hydrating

3.3 Consummation of marriage [18]

The term "Consummation Of Marriage" refers to the first sexual intercourse between newly married couples, typically on their wedding night. Consummation of marriage is often associated with the legal recognition of a marriage, particularly in religious and legal traditions.

---

[18] https://www.marriagetrac.com/why-sexual-intimacy-is-so-important-for-newlyweds/

Why sex is important in relationships? Can a relationship survive without sex?

Yes, sex isn't always necessary, but it is an important part of a healthy and fulfilling marriage.

Some benefits of sex in a relationship are:

1. Feeling closer to your partner
2. Relieving stress
3. Feeling confident
4. Desire to have children
5. Pleasure
6. Showing affection

Sex can play a role in increasing intimacy between romantic partners, regular sex is linked to lower divorce rates among married couples. It is physically and psychological beneficial as it improves sleep, lowers stress and boosts the immune system. Sex can boost happiness and make a couple bond better.

While frequency varies based on a number of factors like, age, marital status, researchers suggest that couples have sex at a minimum of once per week.

Having sex is connected to a range of positive health effects including increased energy, better mood, lower stress, decreased prostate cancer risk etc.

The importance of sex depends on the couple and the individuals. Not everyone needs sex to bond, but some do. Many times, marriages become monotonous and people start looking for love outside of it, this can also be a result of an unhealthy sex life. Hence, sex helps one stay focused on their marriage.

CITATIONS

1. Times of India- June 2, 2023 - How important Is sex in a relationship - very well mind.

Mentally Preparing to Run a Household

04

Let your husband get involved:[19]

If we aren't purposeful about what goes on in our homes, chaos ensues, whether you have kids or not. Someone has to take charge and get things done. Here are some tips for running a home like a business and getting everyone involved to keep the household running smoothly.

1. EFFICIENCY

Prioritise a morning self care routine, productivity isn't something that stems from waking up at 2pm, a good morning routine ensures work gets done and a good lifestyle enhances your overall life experience. Tasks must be organised and divided, this must be communicated and prepared for beforehand. Time must be efficiently managed as well.

2. AESTHETICS

The home defines the lifestyle of an individual. This might be the reason why many people spend fortunes on creating the most beautiful and visually stunning homes. But what makes a home unique is its visual aesthetics and design.

3. EARTH ETHICS

Earth ethics is a call of responsibility to the earth, one that grows out of our debt of gratitude and the earth's fragility. It is this normative call that

---

[19] *https://www.healthline.com/health/preparing-for-fatherhood*

might guide education in its grappling with environmental issues. We can incorporate this into our households by making small changes like

A] using eco paints
B] Investing in energy efficient appliances
C] installing rainwater harvesting

4. FAMILY TIME

Earth ethics is a call of responsibility to the earth, one that grows out of our debt of gratitude and the earth's fragility. It is this normative call that might guide education in its grappling with environmental issues.

A] create time for your kids
B] have after dinner walks together
C] Share family stories and history
D] Plan holidays
E] spend time with the senior citizens

CITATION

1. How to be productive at home- asana
2. How to run a household- wikihow
3. How to understand home aesthetics- address maker
4. Make your home more sustainable- blog constellation
5. Spend time with your family- familiesforlife

4.1   How and what responsibilities to share with spouse

Household chores are a huge part of one's life, which is to be shared with your partner upon marriage. Household work is repetitive, tedious and thankless as a job, it can become a major stressor in a marriage if not dealt with properly. [20]

---

[20] *https://www.babycenter.com/family/house-and-home/dividing-childcare-and-housework-duties-with-your-partner_446*

Inequality in household work distribution can make the burdened partner feel bothered and upset. This can create resentment in the marriage often leading to divorce. The concept of spouses sharing housework equally is crucial to overcoming patriarchal gender rules. A husband doing housework is about establishing equality in a relationship.

1. Communicate the necessity

Let your partner know that you would want to share responsibilities in the household.

2. Give him an ultimatum

Let your husband know that you aren't his caretaker, establish healthy boundaries.

3. Make lists

A list of chores need to be made and divided between the couple, this is the most constructive method of distributing housework between you and your loved ones.

4. Switch roles

Sometimes, just talking about it wont help, switching roles to make him experience what you have to go through will make him more empathetic towards dividing household chores.

5. Do chores together

Splitting chores is fantastic, but doing them together makes a couple spend time together and bond as well.

4.2 Planning for Children

It's become a cliché that you can never really be "ready" to have children. Still, starting a family is a major, life-changing undertaking, and you should take the time to prepare for it.

One must be prepared mentally to bring a new life into this world, because once a parent, always a parent. The first step is to independently decide for oneself if they would want to do this, are you willing to prioritise another human, love them unconditionally even if they have disabilities and illnesses and make sacrifices for them.

If one is in a marriage or relationship, they must speak to their partner about this as it is a life changing decision that will affect both persons involved. Both persons involved must think about how many children they want, what kind of parents they want to be and what kind of parenting style they'd want to follow.

Pregnancy and parenthood will greatly affect one's career, they must think of all these aspects before jumping into parenthood. Parenthood not only affects one's career but also their social life, which needs to be taken into consideration as well.

Be realistic of how parenthood will affect your marriage or relationship, it may increase your bond but this can also not be the case for some parents.

Make a pre-pregnancy "to-do" list. Think about things you would like to do before you start your family, and try to do as many of those things as you can.

Recognize that you will not be able to plan for everything. Unexpected circumstances always arise where pregnancy and parenthood are concerned. Follow the above steps to plan as best you can, but accept that some things are out of your control.

Citation

1. How ready are you to parent a child- Vidya Shankar
2. How to plan for kids - wikihow

4.3 Parenting Responsibilities[21]

Shared parenting responsibilities a reality or a myth in our patriarchal society?

[21] https://discover.rbcroyalbank.com/seven-strategies-for-sharing-parenting-responsibilities/

Tips and strategies for equal and shared parenting responsibilities:

1. Practise a mindset of shared parental responsibility before the baby is born

Put the idea of primary parent aside, and start as an equal partnership before birth. Partners can read up on pregnancy, attend appointments together, shop for their unborn child together.

2. Share childcare duties fairly

Many government and public sector units are now providing paternity leave, which holds key for caring jointly for a child from birth.

There are a lot of ways to do this, it is purely subjective based on the way the family works. In an ideal utopian world it is possible for equally sharing responsibilities between both parents but this is based on the individual's work, social life, family upbringing, personalities and lifestyles. Splitting your time into shifts can help, each partner can allocate tasks and playing with the individuals strengths can help.

3. Baby bonding time

Make sure each parent gets a good share of baby bonding time, dividing household and parenting duties is fine but one must also bond with their child and not see them as a chore.

4. Acceptance

While both of you want to share work, just know you are both separate individuals with different upbringings and approaches towards parenting styles. Deciding this prior to the birth of the baby takes a load off.

5. Keep communication open

Just as your baby develops, so will your parenting evolve. That means your plan for equally shared parenting may need to change from time to time. What may work during the newborn days might not be the same once one or both of you go back to work, for example. There will be times when you may need to compromise on how equally you are able to share certain tasks. Be open and honest with each other about your individual needs and concerns. Ask for help when you need it. Keep a shared family calendar so you both know what's going on with your child's schedule.

4.4 Minimalism concepts

The idea of minimalism usually does not occur easily,, strangely, especially to those who need it - the hoarders: -) In many countries Retail Therapy is prescribed for those in depression to shop till they drop, not knowing that hoarding will require a greater level of intervention to declutter before healing begins. [22]

ENERGY TAKERS

Focusing on the past
Inconsistent sleep
Mess and clutter
Sedentary time
Social media
Overworking
Dehydration
Screen time
Resentment
Negativity
Junk food
The news
Alcohol
Stress
Fear

ENERGY GIVERS

Music
Nature
Resting
Sunlight
Positivity
Gratitude
Hydration
Meditation
Movement
Breathwork
Community
Decluttering
Consistent sleep
Eating whole foods
Learning something new

[22] *https://www.breakthetwitch.com/minimalism/*

4.5 Social Responsibility and Devotion:[23]

The Sanskrit word Seva, which means "selfless service or labour conducted without any notion of return or payback," is used to describe this kind of work. In ancient India, performing Seva was thought to aid one's spiritual development while also enhancing society. This is the skill of giving without expecting anything in return, in which the act of giving is a gift to all parties involved. The art of blessed action is seva.

The spiritual discipline of Seva is unselfish service. It derives from the yoga of action known as karma yoga and the yoga of worship known as bhakti yoga, which is motivated by divine love. It is one of the most straightforward yet powerful and life-altering ways we may put our spiritual understanding into practice.

Making a substantial contribution to the spiritual community of our fellow beings on earth is possible by offering our Seva. It is a spiritual discipline that helps us grow spiritually and a practice that helps us discover the deeper meaning of who we really are. Each and every one of us is a manifestation. Everything makes the divine evident. Service can instil the notion of the fundamental one more strongly than any other action.

Service broadens your perspective, increases your awareness, and deepens your compassion, saving you from the misery you experience when another person suffers. Every wave originates from and is on the same sea. It teaches you to firmly hold onto this understanding. No other sadhana can lead you to a state of constant meditation on the interconnectedness of all living things.

Through the practice of Seva, we have been given a priceless opportunity to grow in devotion, character, humility, and self-abnegation.

---

[23] *https://www.scribd.com/document/443500884/The-Minimalists-16-Rules-for-Living-with-Less*

Financial Prudence

Further Reading: https://prawo.uni.wroc.pl/sites/default/files/students-resources/A%20Brief%20Guide%20to%20Financial%20Freedom.pdf

5.1   Financial prudence[24]

Financial prudence means careful management of available funds or capital in an effective and efficient way. Financial prudence basically means planning well in advance and investing in areas where you can expect high returns. It also means having complete knowledge about the money you have and how you can make it grow best.

Create a monthly budget: Live within your means by creating a budget in the beginning of every month. Stick to this budget and avoid overspending on unnecessary items

Make buying decisions on the VALUE you get: If you are planning to buy a house, or a car or a motorcycle, your decision should be based on the value you get for the same over its entire lifecycle.

Automated monthly transfer to a dedicated savings / contingency account: This is the real trick behind saving. Set a particular amount aside and opt for automated transfer that will help you save for your big buy or for your next holiday or simply for retirement

Avoiding impulse purchases: Don't indulge in an impulsive buy, or try to curb extravagant habits as much as possible.

---

[24] *https://www.moneymanagement.org/budget-guides/combine-your-finances-after-marriage*

Undertake periodic maintenance to avoid higher bills a later stage: What you neglect now, will ask for your attention at a later stage.

Citation

Financially prudent habits- herofincorp.com

5.2   Multiple Sources of Income

You may be used to relying on a single stream of income. But having multiple sources of income can open up all sorts of opportunities for you. Not only does it provide financial security and stability, but it also creates new possibilities for your creativity and career growth.

Having multiple streams of income can help safeguard your finances during times when one source may not be as reliable or lucrative as another. This could be due to seasonal changes in demand or sudden shifts in the economy. Having different sources of income gives you greater flexibility to respond to changing market conditions and helps you build resilience into your business model over time.

Passive income is money earned without actively working. Generally speaking, it leverages existing skills and requires minimal investment. It offers financial freedom and flexibility, supplementing or replacing regular income.

Ways to make extra income

1. Consider moonlighting- working a side gig
2. Sign up for ride sharing service- save money through commuting
3. Small home business- consider catering or making homemade products to make some extra money
4. Make extra income through tutoring- doing this part time can also become a career
5. Renting your extra bedroom- if you've extra space that you aren't using, rent it out to make extra income.

Emotional Readiness

Marriage is a legal and social institution in which two individuals come together, in Indian society it even means the coming together of the two families. Marriage plays a significant role in every married person's life.

Marriage is not a child play. It is an important responsibility requiring a degree of readiness, for it to be successful. Family life which normally comes soon after marriage is even a greater responsibility requiring even greater readiness, to be successful. Readiness is being prepared. Readiness for marriage is preparing individuals for marriage. Being ready for marriage is not just a matter of age. Ideas about the level of readiness needed for marriage differ from culture to culture and within cultures. Different people and individuals are ready for marriage at different times and in different ways. This preparation is not an overnight phenomenon. The preparation for healthy living and happy married and family life begins at an early age in most societies.

Marriage readiness not only means reaching the physical readiness for marriage but also refers to the financial, social and mental readiness for marriage.

Marriage readiness refers to the evaluation and subjective perception of one's own preparedness for the responsibilities and challenges of marriage. It is an important factor in predicting marital satisfaction and future well-being

Psychological readiness for marriage is much more complex and harder to measure than the *physiological readiness*. It is also much more important. Marriage involves intimate relationships and thus, requires sensitivity to interpersonal relations which is possible only when a married couple is psychologically ready for it.

Psychological readiness for marriage means:

- Being able to accept new relations, new roles and necessary adjustments required in it.
- Assuming personal responsibility for one's growth and development.
- Having a healthy attitude towards sex, sexuality and overcoming fears, if any, towards sex, pregnancy, child-birth, in-laws and fear of non-performance among men.

6.1 Psychological factors that affect relationships - how to detect them

PD Mithra - Support Group for Caregivers Coping with Family Member's Personality Disorders.docx

Download the PD Mithra Document from: *awakentolife.org/paid-resources/*

6.2 Self Esteem Improvement

Psycho Cybernetics by Maxwell Maltz - Full Audiobook[25]

---

[25] *https://www.amazon.in/Psycho-Cybernetics-Updated-Expanded-Maxwell-Maltz/dp/0399176136*

Spiritual Ascension

https://anandaindia.org/blog/what-is-spiritual-marriage/

Spiritual marriage means union with God, Soul, and Spirit. Marriage is not a man-made law. It is God-made. Man has abused the high purpose of marriage. Marriage means unity on the physical, mental, and spiritual planes. If you attract a person by spiritual magnetism, then you will meet your soul companion. Marriage is the communion of half-souls. In God we find the highest communion. Unless human love is spiritualized, it will be a canker in your soul. Unless you are spiritually-minded and your mate is the same, you can never be happy.

Spiritual marriage means to marry your soul to the eternal love of God. Without God no marriage can be successful. The purpose of marriage is to know God, to be with God together, but this has been forgotten.

Do not try to attract the opposite sex through physical desires but through soul qualities. You cannot attract a spiritual soul through animal magnetism. Too much living on the sex plane causes health and happiness to fly away. When you have formed a tremendous friendship with a person that nothing can destroy, a friendship that has no compulsion in it and that increases constantly, you have found a true mate.

See also: *https://joyfulearth.org/vishwas/spiritual-processes/*

Vishwas is a support group for people going through a spiritual emergence or process during their mental health crisis and beyond.

7.1   Balancing Reason and Feeling

In women, feeling is expressed uppermost and in man, reason is expressed uppermost. In married life, they bring out the hidden feeling and reason in each other, thus becoming more perfect. Every man and woman who have tried to seek a substitute for that spiritual quality through the sex instinct, have been disappointed. Reason and feeling in man and woman should be balanced. Like the softness of flowers, and the strength of steel, they are divine qualities.

God is all the love of all the lovers who ever loved. If you learn the higher forms of meditation, you can have spiritual marriage, or that communion with God which is the most beautiful of all love. Remember, no marriage can find its true purpose without man and wife first seeking God together. In marriage, love also grows through service to each other. When a husband and wife serve each other with the eternal inspiration of God, that is spiritual marriage.

People who rise above the physical plane and continuously strengthen the love of their souls find their oneness in God. When the love of two persons burns as one flame, above the physical plane, then it has intoxicating eternal qualities. The marriage that is lived in self-control and intense spiritual preparation becomes emancipated.

Man and woman should know that within themselves is the germ of the Infinite. If you cannot find your soul companion, do not marry. If you have found God, you do not need your soul companion. It is better to remain single than to enter into a wrong marriage. Transmute matrimonial love into love divine, and bring back your consciousness from the sex plane to the plane of paradise.

You may unite your feelings and reason by giving yourself to humanity. By having a bigger family, you have the right not to have a smaller, more limited one. For all those who are unmarried and wish to remain so, their greatest duty in life is service to humanity. If you do not marry physically, you must marry spiritually; otherwise you cannot be liberated. If you have no children of your own, adopt or teach the children of someone else, live an ideal life, and instill your soul qualities in them. What you instill in the souls of children is imperishable. Anything you do that perpetuates your life is, in a sense, your child. Thus fulfill your true purpose in life.

7.2 What do ancient scriptures say on the responsibilities of married women? How to interpret it for modern times?

*Kamlesh D Patel

So which one is better - the exciting early days of romance, or the halcyon days of an elderly couple? This seems like a silly question, given that it is obvious they are different stages in the evolution of a marriage, both relevant and both important. It would be a silly question, except for the fact that today most marriages in the West, and an increasing number in the East, do not last the distance. It is often not at the beginning or the end that marriages falter, but midway, when the struggles are the greatest. So what makes the difference between a couple that is able to stay with the evolutionary process of marriage and one that does not? As more and more youngsters look for answers to such questions, where reason and emotions converge, where tradition and contemporary thinking meet, and perhaps, where science and spirituality meet, there is a need for a very relevant and practical approach to relationships that also encompasses the wisdom of the ages.

Some ancient wisdom

In Yogic philosophy, we learn about the three human types: sattvik, rajasic and tamasic. We are all a mixture of the three, but generally one predominates in our make up, and this can change as we evolve.

Tamasic behaviour is characterised by ignorance and inertia. A tamasic person is often lethargic, prone to violence, and mistrust. Rajasic behaviour is characterised by action and passion. A rajasic person is one who is often focused on satisfying his own personal desires, gain and prosperity. Sattvik behaviour is characterised by purity and wisdom. A sattvik person cheerfully serves others without any expectation of personal benefit.

These three qualities pervade everything we do - the way we walk, talk and eat, and even the way we breathe. What happens to our breath when we experience intense anger? The nostrils flare and our breath is long, loud and chaotic; tamasic in nature. On the other hand, when we are in the state of samadhi or deep meditation, our breathing is so quiet and calm that we hardly notice it. It flows so naturally and so effortlessly, which is sattvik in nature. These qualities play out in all our interactions with others, and are very evident in our closest relationships. As a result, marriages are also associated with one of these three types.

A tamasic marriage is based on individual gain. The couple is coming together for benefit. For example, the groom might be focused solely on the financial status of the bride's family, or gaining a trophy wife. Alternatively, the bride might be marrying someone much older for money, status or access to an easy visa. Such marriages are transactional in nature, based on narcissistic or self-centered behaviour, and can easily result in mutual distrust and discord. A spouse is a commodity to provide status, pleasure or service.

Today, many marriages are rajasic, based on mutual love and respect, and also mutual desire and benefit. But though there may be mutual respect, the love is not totally pure and unconditional, as there is expectation. So when the other person is flawed and imperfect, as we all are, there is disappointment and trouble in paradise. A sattvik relationship is one in which the two partners don't think of themselves as individuals, but as one. They cheerfully sacrifice everything for the relationship and each other. There is a wonderful short story by O Henry called "The Gift of the Magi" about such a young couple. In a sattvik marriage there is purity of intent, and no concern about physical deficiencies or financial status. Communion, mutual growth and unconditional love are at the core of the marriage. In sattvik marriages, the best emerges over a period of time, as the family is based on giving and love, and so it is strong. When children come along in a marriage, the focus of the couple shifts from attention on each other to a partnership where the main focus of attention is now on the children. The different personality types will respond in different ways to such a shift. What do you imagine will happen to a person who is self focused, who wants his or her spouse to constantly shower attention? And what will happen to a person who is always happy to give and does not need to be the centre of attention? Here is an example of different responses leading to different results.

Me versus We

Marriage and family life teach us to become more and more giving, if we are willing to commit to the journey. There is a traditional French tale, Beauty and the Beast, in which the beast starts out very tamasic, imprisons the beautiful Belle and locks her away as a prize. But over time the kindness, love and acceptance of Belle transforms him into a handsome, gentle prince. We love these folk tales for the very reason that they kindle something in our unconscious mind that we know is possible.

This is the possibility marriage brings to all of us - the opportunity to grow, refine ourselves and learn to love. Through marriage we can evolve into that sattvik state of communion I saw that day in the elderly couple by the river - so subtle, gentle and full of naturalness. I hope that more of us will have the opportunity to experience such a state.

That is why in 21st century yoga, family life is venerated far more than the celibate life of a monk. It is through the love and sacrifice, the struggles and acceptance, and the willingness to grow that marriage offers that we refine ourselves enough to realise our fullest potential as human beings.[26]

7.3   How couples meditation can strengthen your relationship

Clinically reviewed by *Dr. Chris Mosunic*, PhD, RD, CDCES, MBA

Couples meditation could be the key to strengthening your relationship. Learn about the types of meditation for couples, plus techniques to enhance communication.

- Why meditating as a couple is good for your relationship
- How to practice meditation as a couple
- 6 couples meditation exercises to try
- Couples meditation FAQs

---

[26] *https://www.dailyo.in/lifestyle/marriage-divorce-newly-wed-couple-beauty-and-the-beast-o-henry-the-gift-of-the-magi-20683*

Life can get so busy that it's easy to miss out on quality time with our partners. Couples meditation can help ease this burden because it's about taking a moment to truly connect with each other without distractions or to-do lists. With the right couples *meditation* practice, you can focus on the present to help *strengthen your relationship* or reduce stress in your daily lives.

7.4   Why meditating as a couple is good for your relationship

Meditation has long been used to cultivate *inner peace* and improve *mental clarity*. It can also help reduce stress as well as enhance your self-awareness, focus, and *wellbeing*. Sounds great, right? Well, meditating with your partner can also majorly *benefit you as a couple* helping you stay connected and aligned. Here's how.

Couples meditation can help build emotional bridges

When you meditate together, you create a shared experience. Tuning into a quiet moment together can lead to a *stronger emotional bond* over time, making you feel more connected.

Couples meditation can help to enhance communication

Meditation teaches you to be present and to truly listen without immediately reacting. This can help you communicate better in *your relationship* so you can hear with empathy instead of jumping to conclusions.

Couples meditation can offer a shared stress release

When everything feels *overwhelming*, meditating with your partner can be like choosing to tackle *stress* together. The team effort can make you both feel more supported.

Being present together matters

Life is full of distractions, like the constant notifications or the never-ending list of chores. Meditating together encourages you both to be present, savoring the moment. It's a reminder that sometimes, the most important thing is just being there with each other.

Couples meditation can boost intimacy and connection

Meditating together can lead to deeper *emotional intimacy*. It's about vulnerability, trust, and exploring your inner worlds together.

How to practice meditation as a couple

Pick your spot: Find a quiet place where you won't be disturbed. This could be your living room, bedroom, or a spot in your backyard. Choose a space that feels peaceful to both of you.

Stay comfy: Sitting on a cushion, a chair, or *lying down* can work. Choose a comfortable position so you can focus on the meditation throughout. Matching your position to each other can strengthen your *connection*.

Set a time: Just like date night, agree on a time that works for you both. It could be the morning to kickstart your day or before bed to *wind down*.

Keep it short: Especially at the beginning, aim for shorter sessions of 5 or 10 minutes. As you continue to practice, you can gradually increase the time.

Decide on the kind of practice you'll try: Choose a meditation technique that works for both of you (more on that below), or simply focus on your breath. Experiment and see what feels right for you both.

Check-in: Find a special way to close the meditation — maybe sharing a few *deep breaths* or placing your hand over each other's hearts. Sharing can help you connect, so maybe consider chatting about how it felt for a few minutes post-meditation. Did a particular thought arise? Do you feel more relaxed?

Practice patience: Like anything new, there might be a learning curve. One of you may find it easier to switch off while the other's *mind races*. That's okay. Remember, it's a journey you're both on together.

Use tools: Whether it's *calming background music*, a *guided meditation*, or a timer to keep track, use whatever resources make the process smoother for both of you.

Remember, couples meditation isn't about perfection. It's about spending quality time together, tuning into each other, and strengthening your bond.

7.5 Couples meditation exercises to try

If you're ready to try, there are plenty of couples meditation techniques you can explore. The great thing about meditation is that there's no right or wrong way to do it. Try a few types of couples meditation techniques and poses to see what suits you both best.

7.5.1 Breath awareness meditation

For this practice, you'll both focus on your breathing, observing each inhale and exhale without trying to change it. This technique is straightforward and an excellent way for beginners to start. Plus, synchronizing your breathing can be a powerful way to feel connected with the person you love most.

7.5.2 Guided meditation

Use your favourite guided meditations to guide you both through the process. These might include *visualizations* or *affirmations* you follow. If you're new to meditation, a guide can make the process more accessible.

7.5.3 Loving-kindness meditation

To practice, you'll both focus on developing feelings of compassion and love, first for each other and then expanding outwards to family, friends, and even strangers. *Loving-kindness meditation* is a feel-good meditation that can bring positive emotions and deepen your bond.

7.5.4 Body scan meditation

This technique has you mentally scan your bodies from head to toe, noting any sensations, tensions, or relaxation. *Body scan meditation* is a great way to tune into your body, bringing calm after a long day.

7.5.5 Mindfulness meditation

For this practice, you both pay attention to your current experiences—your environment, thoughts, or feelings—without judgement. Mindful acceptance *has been shown* to help improve relationship satisfaction. *Mindfulness* helps train your mind to stay in the present moment, making everyday activities (like that evening walk or cooking dinner together) more enjoyable and meaningful.

7.5.6 Silent gazing meditation

This practice can be really bonding and special. You sit facing each other, gazing into each other's eyes without speaking. While it might feel awkward initially, it can lead to a profound sense of connection and understanding.

7.6 Couples meditation FAQs

Is it good for couples to meditate together?

Meditating together can be a fantastic way for couples to bond on a deeper level and help increase their overall *happiness*. Firstly, you both get the individual *benefits of meditation*, like reduced stress and increased mindfulness. Secondly—and more importantly—doing it together can enhance communication, foster mutual empathy, and create shared experiences that strengthen the relationship.

How to approach the subject of meditation with a partner?

Just like introducing any new idea, start the conversation light and open. Share your experiences or what you've read about the benefits of couples meditation. Express how it might be a fun bonding activity to try together and be receptive to your partner's thoughts and *feelings*. Remember, it's not about convincing but sharing something that could benefit you both.

What is intimate meditation?

Intimate meditation is about blending mindfulness with emotional or physical intimacy. It's about being truly present with each other. This could involve maintaining eye contact, synchronized *breathing*, or sitting silently together. It's all about feeling connected on a deeper level.

How do you meditate in a relationship?

Everyone's different, so even in a relationship, *meditation* can be a unique experience for each person. Try other techniques, or start with shorter sessions, and if one of you finds it challenging, be patient and supportive. Make it a joint journey of exploration and learning.

How to get the most out of meditation with your partner?

Try a few different techniques to find something that fits your needs and that you both enjoy. At the end of the day it's all about what will enhance your connection and reduce your collective stress.

Stress less, sleep more, and feel better with Calm.

7.7 Awareness and Attitude

Premarital counselling can help couples identify differences and learn to be more self-aware and compromising. Open and honest communication can help couples build trust, enhance intimacy, and prevent misunderstandings from escalating into conflicts.

Here are some tips for improving your relationship:

- Communicate clearly: Communicate often and share your innermost wishes, fantasies, and desires with your partner.
- Have a positive attitude: A positive attitude can help you enjoy each other's company and be less critical.
- Focus on the small moments: Create rituals to build the life you want in your relationship.
- Learn to forgive: Understand that it's OK to disagree.
- Make time for you two: Surround yourselves with people in healthy relationships.
- Be compassionate: Assume the best.

You can also try these strategies to help solve marriage problems:

- Act as if your spouse's happiness is more important than your own.
- Put the relationship ahead of everything, including your children.
- Stop taking one-another for granted.
- Experiment with new ways to bring pleasure to each other.
- Look at sex as an opportunity to get to know your partner better over time

7.8   Stemming of Genuine Concerns[27]

The first gaps start showing up when there is lack of clarity in communication and expectations.

How do you fix communication problems in marriage?

Effective *communication in marriage* may not be intuitive for everyone. For many of us, it's a skill set that takes some know-how. Here's how to get started:

Process your feelings

You may find it helpful to take a moment and sort through your feelings ahead of time. This could look like:

- journaling stream of consciousness
- observing your thoughts in meditation
- practising what you want to say in a mirror
- writing a "vent" letter (that you don't send!)

Create a 'container'

You can *pick a time and a place*, preferably when both of you won't be rushed or distracted. From there, you might try this process:

1. Put your phones on silent.
2. Relax your body language to signal "openness."
3. Lay down some ground rules, like no interrupting or raising your voice.
4. Set a timer for a previously agreed upon amount of time.
5. Stick to the topic at hand — and only that topic.
6. *Avoid complaining* and blaming.
7. Use "I" statements (e.g., "I feel sad when I cook dinner and end up eating it alone").

---

[27] *https://www.marriage.com/advice/pre-marriage/premarital-counseling-questionnaire/*

8. While you're silent, hone your *active listening skills.*

9. When the timer goes off, reset it so the other person can speak.

7.9   Understanding Wedding Vows[28]

What are Wedding Vows? Here's Everything You Need to Know

Wondering what are wedding vows? This guide explains everything you need to know about the exchange of vows and how they differ based on religion.

Nora Shepard

We've seen it in *a million wedding movies*—during the ceremony, a couple recites a bunch of words to each other, ending in "'til death do us part", then they kiss, and are officially married. But what are wedding vows and why do couples have to recite them during the ceremony? And what's the deal with writing your own wedding vows—can you actually do that? We're here to help answer all of your wedding-vow-related questions, and help figure out which type of wedding vow is right for your big day. So, what are wedding vows? Get ready for your crash course!

Wedding Vows 101

So, what are wedding vows? Most simply, marriage vows are the promises two people make to each other during a wedding ceremony. These promises can look different across religions, as well as from couple to couple. You're basically declaring your lifelong commitment to your spouse, witnessed by your loved ones (*here are some examples!*). Vows can be romantic and emotional, of course, but can also be humorous—it all depends on your style and the structure of your ceremony, as determined by your officiant.

Vows typically take place after your officiant's sermon or any religious readings you choose to have. You will generally exchange rings immediately following the vows, with the pronouncement of marriage and the kiss following that.

---

[28] *https://psychcentral.com/health/marriage-communication-common-mistakes-and-how-to-fix-them#solutions*

You may be most familiar with the traditional Catholic wedding vows (these are the ones most commonly recited in movies): "I, [name], take you, [partner's name], for my lawful wife/husband, to have and to hold from this day forward, for better, for worse, for richer, for poorer, in sickness and health, until death do us part."

Wedding vows can be recited in three different ways. If you and your partner write your own vows, you will be speaking directly to one another.

Another option is to repeat the vows after your officiant, which can alleviate some of the pressure associated with reciting vows. For example:

Officiant: "Please repeat after me. I, Laura, take thee, Susan,"

Laura: "I, Laura, take thee, Susan."

Your third option to declare, "I do," to your officiant who recites vows in a question-answer format. For example:

Officiant: "Do you, Cameron, you take this man to be your lawfully wedded groom?"

Cameron: "I do."

How do wedding vows differ across religions and cultures?

Catholic

There are two sets of *American Catholic wedding vows* that are approved by the Vatican—work with your priest to determine which one is best for you and your ceremony. If you're hosting a Catholic wedding, it's unlikely that you will be able to write your own vows.

Jewish

Traditionally, there is no exchange of vows in *a Jewish ceremony* – the wedding ritual presumes the promises. The vows occur when the groom puts the ring on his partner's finger and utters the words, "you are consecrated to me with this ring according to the laws of Moses and Israel."

Protestant

Each of the different Protestant churches has its own wedding vows. Whether you're Episcopalian, Methodist, Presbyterian, or Lutheran, you'll want to talk to your officiant to find out the appropriate vows for your denomination.

Hindu

One of the most important *Hindu wedding rituals* is Saptapati, or Seven Steps. These are promises that the couple makes to each other as they enter into marriage.

Muslim

Most *Muslim ceremonies* do not include vows. The couple will typically listen to their imam's words about marriage, and are then asked if they accept the terms of their marriage. In some cases, Muslim couples can recite vows to each other.

Eastern Orthodox

In most Eastern Orthodox traditions, no vows are spoken during the ceremony. Symbolic rituals are used in place of the spoken vows.

Unitarian

Unitarian wedding vows can be fairly flexible and left up to the minister to determine the exact wording.

7.10   Wedding Vows - FAQs

What is the declaration of intent?

Once you and your partner have made promises to each other in the form of vows, there's another part of the ceremony—the declaration of intent. Especially if you are writing your own vows, it's important to keep in mind that the declaration of intent is legally required to pronounce you married. The vows are comprised of promises, but the declaration typically follows right after the vows. It's when the couple takes each other's hands and exchange the "I do's." The officiant prompts the two lovebirds, and the bride and groom (or bride and bride, or groom and groom), respond with "I do," or sometimes, an "I will." It should go without saying, but you should plan this part of the wedding in advance with your officiant.

Should we write our own vows?

While writing your own vows is a great way to *personalize your ceremony*, you don't have to go this route. In particular, if you're having a religious ceremony that has a stricter ceremony script and structure, you may not be able to personalize your vows. If writing your vows is really important to you and you can't make it part of your official ceremony, feel free to do a separate, more intimate ceremony where you declare your own vows – it can even be just you and your partner, before or after the larger ceremony. You're making the promise to cherish your partner forever, and most importantly, that should never be taken lightly.

Is it okay to read your personal wedding vows as opposed to memorizing them?

While it's certainly preferable to memorize your wedding vows, we actually recommend having a copy of your vows in hand at your ceremony so you can read them if need be. Unless you're a professional performer or are adept at public speaking, you'll probably be pretty nervous before reciting your vows—so it's better to have a printed copy of your vows in front of you for easy access. You can even write your vows (neatly!) in a designated *vow book* to add a prettier, personalized touch.

How long should wedding vows be?

When recited out loud, wedding vows should be between one and two minutes long—which is about 100 to 200 words when read at a slow pace. To test out how long your vows will be, practice reading them aloud in front of a mirror (loudly, slowly, and clearly, please) and adjust the text length accordingly.

Do you have to say your vows in front of everyone?

If you like the idea of writing personal vows to your partner but are terrified at the thought of reciting them in front of all of your loved ones, fear not! You can simply repeat the standard vows after your officiant, and recite your personal vows in a more private setting—for example, during your first look or after the ceremony. If you're okay reciting your personal vows in front of a smaller group, you might opt to do an informal exchange of vows at your rehearsal dinner.

7.11   Deeper Understanding of Life

Here are some ways to develop a deeper understanding of life with your partner:

Empathy

Helps you understand your partner's point of view, both their successes and struggles.

Appreciation

Research shows couples who express gratitude and appreciation feel more connected, loving, and satisfied in their relationships.

Quality time

Helps foster connection, intimacy, and understanding.

Communication

Helps couples create a deeper understanding of each other, including their thoughts, feelings, needs, and wants.

Trust

When trust is strong, partners feel more comfortable expressing their needs, desires, and emotions, leading to a deeper understanding of one another.

Pregnancy, Delivery and Parenting 08

8.1 Conception

Conscious Conception: Your Journey to Motherhood

Parenting begins before birth. This includes prenatal maternal and paternal bonding with the baby, and biological effects on foetal development. Recent research has confirmed how prenatal maternal stress can alter the development of the foetus and the child, and that this can persist until early adulthood. Children are affected in different ways depending, in part, on their own genetic makeup. The foetus may also have a direct effect on prenatal maternal mood and later parenting behaviour via the placenta. The father is important prenatally too. An abusive partner can increase the mother's prenatal stress and alter foetal development, but he can also be an important source of *emotional support*. New research suggests the potential benefits of prenatal interventions, including viewing of prenatal scans and *cognitive behavioural therapy*.

8.1.1 Introduction

Parents can alter the development of their child, even before birth. Several different ways in which this can occur will be discussed in this review. The mother's emotional state during pregnancy can have a direct influence on foetal development by foetal programming.

Her obesity can also alter the development of her foetus and child. The mother's emotional state during pregnancy is a predictor of her mood postnatally, so if she is depressed prenatally she is at strong risk of being depressed postnatally, and this can also have an effect on her parenting. The partner has a major part to play during pregnancy, especially by his or her effects on the mother's emotional state.

An abusive partner can be very detrimental to a woman's prenatal emotional state, whereas a supportive partner may buffer her against depression or anxiety. The feelings of bonding or attachment between a parent and baby can start prenatally, and continue after the baby is born. Again this is mostly observed between the mother and her unborn child, but the father can start to have feelings of attachment prenatally.

It is well known that maternal smoking, alcohol and drug consumption during pregnancy can affect foetal development. However, evidence from animal studies suggests that paternal alcohol consumption may also have an effect on the offspring, reducing cognitive development, and increasing anxiety and depression, via epigenetic changes in the sperm. Most of the research on these topics has been psychological, but the underlying biology is starting to be explored, as are interventions that start in pregnancy and can help child outcomes.

8.1.2 Maternal mood in pregnancy:

Women have as many symptoms of depression and anxiety during pregnancy as they do postnatally. These can have a direct effect on the development of her baby as can other experiences of stress, including exposure to natural disasters or to man-made traumas. Many women have pregnancy specific anxiety, an especial concern about the outcome of their pregnancy, and some recent studies have revealed.

8.1.3 Foetal programming:

Foetal programming is the concept that the environment in the womb, during different sensitive periods for specific outcomes, can alter the development of the foetus, with a long lasting effect on the child. If the mother is stressed, anxious or depressed whilst she is pregnant, this can have a direct effect on the development of her foetus. The child is somewhat more likely to be born smaller for the gestational age, and also to be born earlier. Essentially, foetal programming refers to the process of sustaining or affecting a stimulus or impairment that occurs at a crucial point in its development. Read more at:[29]

---

[29] *https://www.ncbi.nlm.nih.gov/pmc/articles/PMC5694724/#:~:text=Fetal%20 programming%20occurs%20during%20embryonic,metabolic%20functions%20of%20 the%20fetus*

8.1.4 Prenatal attachment or bonding

There is good evidence that a mother can start to bond with her baby while she is pregnant and that this can continue into her relationship with her baby after birth. For example Rossen et al. have shown that higher prenatal bonding predicted higher postnatal bonding, and that maternal depressive symptoms in trimesters two and three were related to poorer mother-infant bonding 8 weeks postnatally.

8.1.5 Obesity

Maternal obesity is also associated with altered outcome for her child. High pre pregnancy BMI has been shown to increase the risk of her child having symptoms of ADHD and emotional difficulties. Additionally, de Vries et al. found that high pre pregnancy BMI increased the risk of the baby developing a wheeze. Both maternal and paternal pre pregnancy obesity have been found to be associated with an altered epigenetic pattern in the baby's cord blood.

8.1.6 Fathers

The partner is very important in relation to the mother's feelings of stress, and this can affect the development of her foetus. Mothers who said that their partner was emotionally cruel to them had children more likely to score less well cognitively, and to show more fear reactivity, even when a range of other potential confounders, including postnatal experience, were taken into account. The mood of the father during pregnancy is important also..

8.1.7 Underlying biology

The biological mechanisms that underlie foetal programming, and possibly some of the other aspects of prenatal parenting such as prenatal bonding, are only just starting to be understood. We do not know what changes in the mother are most important for mediating the effects of her prenatal mood on foetal development.

8.1.8 Interventions

All this suggests that interventions with the parents to improve child outcome should start before birth. Both Pavlova et al. and de Jong-Pleij et al. have shown that viewing ultrasound scans had a positive impact on prenatal maternal-foetal bonding. Rather few interventions have started during pregnancy and followed the outcome for the child, but those that do show promise.

8.1.9 Conclusion

Parenting begins before birth. The emotional state of the pregnant woman can affect her child by foetal programming, by prenatal bonding, and via links with her postnatal mood and parenting. The father is an important determinant of the mother's emotional state too. For the best outcomes for our children we need to start to provide appropriate help to both parents prenatally, especially for those who are most vulnerable.[30]

Further Reading: conscious_conception_guide.pdf

8.2 Pregnancy and Delivery

Natural birthing

Sangheetha Parthasarathy – World Doula

Should we become parents?

There is a lot of doubt-stream effect of men and women going through the conveyor belt, not just in education but also through out life- including going to college, finding a job, being out there in the job market, wanting to get married by a certain time, to a certain kind of person. Then there is pressure to conceive. There is a large part of life that we all go through without questioning things! Parenting is not something to be taken lightly. There are deep consequences to having a child – without being ready.

Should we become parents - is a question to place on the table, along with the how and when.

---

[30] *https://www.sciencedirect.com/science/article/abs/pii/S2352250X16301671*

What is autonomy and Conscious Conception? We all carry conscious imprints on how we were conceived. Was there joy, volition, was I wanted, not wanted? These are carried in our bodies as somatic imprints. Can you recollect what was in your first year of life? We cannot remember.

The part of the brain that takes our bodily experience and converts them into memory, stores them in the cabinet called hippocampus. This doesn't stream in till about 18 months. But, just because we cannot verbalize those experiences doesn't mean we don't remember. Those are the somatic imprints also called pre-verbal memories, stored as instinct, emotion, movements, in our cells of what happened during conception and in-utero experiences.

When there is autonomy in the decision considering a human need rather than any coercion or benefits – the intention of conception of both the parents, to procreate and bring life into the world.

Bringing a baby into the world is unfortunately seen as a woman's job as the society's perception is that the male's job is done after he deposits the sperm. There is unfair pressure on the women, because on the one hand, we just don't know how to support them and if that is not enough, we end up guilt tripping and shaming them on whatever happens during pregnancy and childbirth!

But to give a sense of this, when we are in – utero, we are connected to our mother, there is an umbilical cord and there are two layers of support- much symbolic on how our societies are created – centred around the newborn, as the mother holds the child. A network of people holds her, so she can do the mothering job. In today's world, both parents are involved from the very beginning and a whole lot of friends and relatives come around to support them. In that sense, mothers are our first wombs after we enter the world.

The two universal experiences are birth and death which all of us go through, whether you want to become parents or not. So we carry these imprints going forward, into our relationships, how we find who we fall in love, besides when we bring another life into this world.

This two layered support is crucial, and it is important for us to understand how to get that support going for us when we prepare to conceive. These conversations are very important to have.

Why does the way you are born matter?

We are meant to be conceived and birthed in love. The love hormone – Oxytocin is a shy bonding hormone which both men and women secrete for conception to happen. We need lots of this hormone for natural labor to start and progress on its own. But we know that Oxytocin is shy, so we need conditions of connection and protection around us, for it to be produced.

When your body produces this hormone naturally, it kickstarts a whole lot of hormonal and neurological changes in the mother and baby towards preparation for birth. Synthetic oxytocin is what is used for inducing. It does not cross your blood brain barrier. Only natural oxytocin can cross that and prepare the mother for nurturing and maternal and bonding behavior.

This hormone also sets off a series of chemical reactions in the baby that cause the baby's sense of smell to mature. Why is that important? As soon as the baby is born, they will smell the mother's breast and move towards it to suckle on it immediately, which in turn brings a whole array of psychological and immunological processes. We are all thinking of birth as a clinical event, that a mother goes through and that a live mother and live baby are the holy grail of the birthing experience. We leave out the baby in the process, who is actually birthing himself, and not the mother.

They need to make 7 movements towards your pelvis and when they do that, it would synthesize their integrated movement, coordination and all of those parameters that ensure independence for the child, later. The feeling of autonomy, that "I did it" will be the lasting imprint for the baby. This is important in so many different perspectives for the baby.

I want you to imagine this from the baby's perspective; they had been housed thus far in a comfortable, warm home, the first imprint of the world on entry, would come with the seeking of security, "whether I will be received well and met with love. Am I going to be heard, seen and kept comfortable?"

Why do we need to birth in love?

The trauma of mothers is that they don't get to hold the baby right after the baby is born, or feed him the colostrum, and had to watch formula being given without her consent! The baby gets sleepy, doesn't latch on later, has initial bonding difficulty, a whole cascade of things happen from conception to the birthing and beyond.

In today's world, the whole outer network of support for the couple influences every decision about the child. However, if this network is between the couple then it is a crowded marriage that will expect you to build your case and seek validation each stage from conception to delivery later on to schooling and life after too, which would be a loss of autonomy for the parents, as we would have not known how to draw the line and get independent, respectfully without depending on them for favors etc.

That a baby will bring a couple closer together is not true. Having a child is like holding a magnifying glass in a relationship. Unless you have a strong relationship between spouses, the testing times during the birthing process and post natal care, will wear down individuals. By birthing in love, is giving the child, the best start in life for early attachment, a feeling of safety. The more natural birthing one has, the more bonding does result for your child's overall wellbeing throughout life. Attachment forms the basis of every neurological basis after that.

The 3 parts of the brains – primitive part- the reptilian one which scans the environment for safety – the brain stem – there is no learning without this.

Next is the mammalian brain – where the limbic system operates – about feelings

The last part is the neocortex, the rational analytical part of the brain. For an infant the neocortex is not fully developed. So they are very instinctual beings. Will I be met if I reach out – the caregiver impressions. Birthing has a huge implication on the child's sense of safety.

We are birthing in violence – no wonder there are so many angry children out there. If we heal birthing, we can heal the world! Oxytocin, natural is needed for happy birthing. Nature is intelligent, will make the two involved parties adequately prepared. But now we are in a stage of society where we can conceive without oxytocin, and birth without it in c section or with synthetic one injected. Artificial formula from day of birth, without breast milk etc – has a huge impact on our abilities to bond, our abilities to love etc. When we mess with birth, we mess with millions of years of evolution – like no other living process.

Early attachment is so important- it is much more than filling the stomach. The survival instinct repeatedly coming over them. It has a huge impact on mothers too.

Normal delivery- is not normal when it is in a hospital.

- C Section
- In labor- C section
- Assisted vaginal birth
- Natural birth

Not more than 10 to 15 pc should be C section to save the life of mothers.

Big city hospitals – 90 pc C section and births are randomly medicalized.

What are the natural choices?:

- Hospital care, working with doulas as a team, and facilitate natural births
- Midwifery led care – they are guardians of normality in a birth. They are trained to place importance on physiology. This is the best option.

Home birth midwifery is not allowed in many states. Birth is institutionalized. Good preparation towards holds key for a great birthing experience.

The choice of birthing is not considered as much as choices that revolves around clothing or wedding.

This being a life project, we should consider their safe future.

Classes in hospitals do not reveal much or education about your body or options available as it would amount to losing their business.

Hypnobirthing works on the mind and body connection. The fear attached to child birthing is never removed, it is in the unconscious. The whole picture needs to be given to the mother, including exercises and preparation. Gentle birth is a good app for pregnant people to download.

- Mobility
- Upright positions

Many other factors need to be considered to unlearn past fears and choosing the right care provider. If they have unprocessed trauma or very low experience in the country where you are in, they aren't good ones. How updated they are on the recent developments in natural birthing. How are they going to be seeing and meeting you where you are! It will help you decide.

8.3   Early Parents

Before conception – prenatal preparation on mental readiness, responsibilities of both parents and resources needed for bringing up the baby into a productive, happy and confident adult.

The preparedness is towards mindful parenting, where the parents actually perform their role, to the best of their abilities, after becoming aware of the responsibilities in having a baby. If we need to fulfill our promise of being prepared parents, willing to take full responsibility from an informed decision of conception to natural delivery, then, awareness on child development and our duties towards the child at each stage, holds the key. It is the right of a child – to have prepared parents, which many of us are not aware of!

1. Before planning to conceive, it is good to know what is expected of parents.

    - Having a child is a long term project. Once you're a parent, the role is irreversible.

- Every child has the right to have good role models of both genders. Hence both parents need to make their presence felt with tangible roles and dividing of duties.
- Role of each parent will change as the baby grows and this has to be woven into daily life by understanding the child's growing needs.
- Frank conversations on birthing, child upbringing and freedom will have to be had with kin staying with you, and extended family, wherever necessary, so that conflicts are minimized within the family.
- In the best interest of the child and the mother, the father needs to be physically and mentally available at every stage of pregnancy, during delivery, and for partnering in the parenting process thereafter.
- The child arrives as a hope for mankind, a teacher for the future and hence we need to hold reverence for his being from conception itself.
- Learning about the needs of the child, at each stage, in the womb and after birth, besides the process that the mother has to go through during pregnancy will be a good preparation.
- Many cultures have certain auspicious rituals for welcoming the baby in the womb and thereafter. These should be discussed within the family and conducted with the presence of both parents.
- It is necessary and ideal that the residence of the child is not altered for the first 3 years.
- Both parents need to understand the promise of conscious parenthood and shared partnership in bringing up the child.

The options available for the birth, the processes before can all be learnt during this time itself. These need to cover what work/travel arrangements are agreed upon by the couple.

- Usually families recommend hospital birth, visiting a local known or referred gynaecologist. There are other options available now.
- Birthing centres that are run by Doula's and birthing assistants with an emergency hospital tie up for necessity are blossoming these days.

Ex

- Birthvillage, Kochi
- Blooms Birthing Centre, Chennai
- Sanctum, Hyderabad.
- The Birth Home, Bengaluru.

Birthing educators and Hypno birthing therapists provide wonderful services to pregnant mothers. Classes are also conducted for parents to understand the steps in happy and comfortable birthing.

2. Once conception is known, the birth plan for the couple must be worked out.

They need to decide their preferred birth mode/location and work on how to go about the birthing process.

- When do we go to the doctor? Only when there is a disease or a malfunction in the body.
- When we are really hungry, we eat our food, this is a natural body function.
- We don't need a doctor to help us satisfy hunger.
- Birthing is also a natural body function.
- Each woman's body is designed to help her deliver a baby, naturally.
- When we trust our body for all our regular natural functions, it is important that we also trust our body for this miracle of birth.
- Doctors may be needed only for rare complications.
- Otherwise, if the parents are well prepared and trust their own bodies, natural birthing with optimal help from experienced midwives, is very much possible.
- Why is natural birthing important?
  - Mother nature is intelligent, birthing is meant to be conscious, joyful, comfortable, and full of love. Healing the past is crucial for a happy birthing.
  - The psychological aspects of the mother and the child is best taken care of in the process of natural birthing. When the

mother delivers the baby, it is like separating an integral part of her own body. It is important for the separated part to be an extension of the original body, for sometime after birth. This is possible by retaining the Umbilical cord and providing for skin to skin contact by the mother immediately after birth. These steps provide vital enrichment for the baby without the trauma of separation from the mother in an alien surrounding.

- ○ The umbilical cord will shrink and wither away on its own and can be removed later on

- ○ These conditions are usually not considered in a hospital environment, where only the adults' convenience is considered. Unless the doctor delivering the baby is cognizant of these requirements, hospital deliveries may not be advantageous for the family, particularly the baby.

- ○ Birthing has to be a pleasant experience for the mother. The physical pain and strain being undeniable, the strength and comfort provided by her husband and the extended family for her birthing journey is crucial for her confidence and overall wellbeing.

- ○ The role of the father must be discussed clearly.

- ○ Parents must be open to change doctors if they do not feel cooperation on these important aspects.

- ○ An understanding birthing assistant (doctor or midwife) should be arrived at very soon so that there is discussion and guidance through the months ahead.

- ○ Considering all of the above, in conjunction of the beliefs of the parents-to-be, the couple must arrive upon a birthing plan, well ahead of time, say by the 5th month into pregnancy.

- • The upcoming 3-5 years will have to be more family centered in the father's life. The mother has to be given the idea that leaving a corporate job is not about giving up a career. It is a period when she is laying the foundation for a well-knit family that is going to have a life long relationship. She can focus on household work and read a lot to learn a lot of things during this time. That the child is a dependent being, and needs our full care and attention is indisputable. We will be taking up the topic related to mothers resuming her career in a later audio clip.

3. Home environment set up:

- Fathers will have to help the mother to clean up the home environment slowly over the conception period, while making the place a happy one for the mother during this time. Setting up of the home environment needs careful consideration by all adults in the home.
- A room for the baby and the mother, that is dimly lit, for the first 8 weeks, is important. This room should also have allocated and carefully equipped places for sleeping, feeding, changing and bathing.
- While this happens, the entire house must be systematically de-cluttered of redundant materials.
- Parents may also involve their time in preparing topponchinos, (soft small elliptical bed for the child to be carried around) vests, cloth nappies, for the child, either at home or by a tailor.
- Movables tied to a string of different types can also be made ready. The changing area must also have a place for temporarily storing soiled cloth, diapers, to wash and sanitize periodically.
- This preparation holds till the child becomes 4 months or moves, whichever is earlier.
- For knowing more about the string mobiles, vests that the babies can wear, the home environment set up, topponchinos please get in touch with us or with an Assistance to Infancy Montessori diploma.

Connecting to the baby in the womb.

- Talking to the baby in the womb is very important. The voice of each adult speaking to the child in the womb will be a comforting reference point after the child is born, and hears sounds in the environment.

The father, mother and maybe a sibling or a grandparent who will be staying with the child after birth, should spend some time each day, talking a few words or sentences, or singing to the child.

Mother could listen to a lot of calming music that is played in the environment, or she herself should sing melodiously. This would be a comforting link after birth.

The mother can also enjoy dance performances or demonstrations of art and music by artists.

We should tell the child that the world is waiting for her/him. Voice recognition is possible with vibrations from the voice that will be sensed by the foetus in the womb.

Rituals that mark the sensorial awakening marked by tinkling of the glass bangles by the mother, is an auspicious celebration called Valaikappu that should be taking place in the 3rd to 4th month, as it is the time when sounds are registered in the forming auditory apparatus of the foetus. These rituals are also helping the mother feel happy and make her presence known in the household for members to reachout to her if she needs help.

- Spiritual preparation on human progress is needed for the mother to accept both happy and grievous events happening around her during this time, with equanimity.
- Movement is crucial for the pregnant mothers, hence yoga and breathing exercises are all good for the muscles to aid delivery. Squatting on the floor and lying on a floor mat for sleeping greatly aids the delivery sphincter muscles. Repeated prostration as an exercise or in reverence, is useful for stretching the perineum, the tissue that expands the most during delivery
- Regular nutritious food, sleep and rhythm is important for the mother. Companionship with the husband to share anxieties and expectations, greatly reduces the delivery angst for the mother, who looks forward to the post- delivery joys.
- Outdoor walks and exercises can be planned in places, that the mother finds peace and calm, like in gardens, parks and beaches and places of worship.

- Food cravings of the mother is expected during pregnancy, and it is a good idea to note down what the foods are, so that it helps during the weaning period of the child.
- A rich sensorial environment for the mother will be the touch-point reference for the baby after birth.
- The manner in which the father cares for the mother by touch and caress, has a positive tactile influence on the baby.
- It is important to maintain positivity and pleasantness throughout the pregnancy time, for the mother, which should be carefully monitored by all adults around.
- When the mother is working on tasks around the home, a strong mental connection even in the subconscious on the presence of her baby within makes the child feel wanted and loved.
- The mother can pursue a new skill in any of the art forms that she feels drawn to, during this period of time.
- The most important cautionary note here is – avoidance of gadgets completely, as it has a negative impact in the foetus's neurological development.

4. During birth Today I will be sharing about the time period closer to birthing. The following is an extract from the book Understanding the Human Being by Dr. Silvana Quattrocchi Montanaro.

It is important to consider how carefully the moment of birth is prepared so that this crucial passage can occur in the best possible way. The Foetus displays all the characteristics of a very attentive traveller, who wishes to arrive at a new place, equipped with all that might be useful to life in the new environment.

The foetus shows a mysterious but accurate intelligence, both biological and psychological, which makes him/her able to evaluate "the date and route" of his/ her travel. By the end of the 7th month of prenatal life, the child attains a level of development that would allow for survival out of the mother's womb (without special technology) and it is precisely at this point, that the child starts "packing its bags".

This is demonstrated in the following ways:

- The child starts to accumulate antibodies from the mother, because it knows that there will be microbes and viruses outside.
- A reserve form of iron is prepared because the child knows that milk will be his only food for many months and that the milk lacks the iron needed for producing the red blood cells.
- The child's head rotates downwards and becomes better oriented towards the birth canal.
- A good quantity of fat is deposited under the skin in preparation for the shift from an environment where the temperature is constant to one where there maybe significant differences in temperature.
- The foetal movements become stronger and more frequent and the volume of the uterus grows very much during this last period of pregnancy. All of this focuses the mother's attention on the child and reminds her of the reality of birth.
- The child is coming and she must prepare herself to be ready to receive him.
- The foetal sleep pattern becomes more similar to the mother's solar rhythm, preparing the child to enter our timescale with its division into day and night.
- Considering all that goes on in the prenatal life, we cannot but admire the intelligent work of the biological and psychological ego of the child. We become aware of the necessity of taking every possible care, inorder to offer the foetus the opportunity to pass from internal to external life as a part of the continuum of development. It is the child himself who prepares for the important change and he should find all the other persons around- mother, father, doctors, nurses etc, prepared to meet his needs. We all must understand the richness and complexity of foetal life, especially the parents. With this knowledge and with our love for the child, we can then prepare ourselves for the important moment of birth.

It is considered that a child can be delivered using induced births, inorder to advance deliveries inorder to coincide with a good birth star, which is on the increase. The after and long term effects of such birthing on the child have been succinctly studied by psychologists and psychiatrists, who see these children in various stages of their lives. (BOX THIS ITEM)

What else we need to prepare as the date is approaching.

A month before the due date, parents can get ready a birthing kit. This can contain

- A topponchino
- A small covering cloth
- Few cloth nappies
- Few vests
- Changing clothes for the mother
- Cleaning and hygiene kit for the mother
- Towels as needed
- Changing sets and hygiene kit for the person accompanying
- Flask
- Plate, Cup and spoon for the mother, and for the accompanying set- 1 each
- Powder
- An old soft plain pure light coloured cotton sari for the baby.
- Bits of small soft cloths for wiping meconium will be idea.

The birthing assistant – either the doctor or the midwife must be available on call to attend to the delivery at anytime of the day or night. Mental strength of the mother to understand and expand her pain bearing capacity holds the key to a successful delivery. Hastening of the pain using hormonal injections or giving anaema to the mother must be avoided. Contractions towards delivery can go on from anywhere between 3 hours to 72 hours and the baby will decide when to come out, until which the pain will increase on a trajectory, the crescendo period the highest pain time, restricted to the last few minutes of arrival provided the birthing position is proper. This information would give the mother strength to believe in her own capacity to bring forth her baby with all the needed preparation.

There are many hospitals who allow husbands to be present at the time of delivery and you can say that the husbands must make use of that offer and attend.

Signs of birthing.:

Today I am going to talk about the actual birthing process. It would be ideal for both parents to listen to this clip and share their thoughts. Given that the parents have been following the prescribed good birthing practices advised to them from the birthing centre, it will be expected that the hotline emergency will respond to their call, to pursue the birthing process to fruition. I shall explain a little in detail about the birthing process.

There are 3 periods in birthing.

1) The dilation period,
2) The expulsive period
3) The expulsion of foetal membranes.

Dilation period lasts between 2 to 20 hours, based on if this is the first birth or second. There are again 3 parts in this dilation period.

a) The early part, where the dilation is 0 to 4 cms of the cervical opening, this may occur for a few hours or even a few days.
b) Active labor is 5 to 7 cms dilation
c) Transition period 7 to 10 cms dilation.

The time varies depending on the mother, but progressively gets shortened.

The expulsive period. This lasts from 1 to 3 hours. The timings could vary based on the birth order and preparation of the expanding muscles's elasticity due to regular exercising.

The expulsion of foetal membranes. Upto 30 minutes after the child has come out.

The signals of readiness towards delivery, is the marked by the release of the Oxytocin hormone, from the pituitary gland that triggers the involuntary contractions of the uterus. This initiates the process of labour.

- During the beginning of the dilation period, contractions last for 15 to 20 seconds, at intervals of 20 to 30 minutes.
- As the dilation period continues, the contractions lengthen into 30 to 50 seconds and intervals shortened to 5 to 10 min.
- Towards the end of the dilation period, the contractions will be 50 to 90 seconds long and the intervals will be 3 to 4 min,

The intervals between the contractions are needed for blood circulation between the mother and the child. Natural oxytocin released by the pituitary gland is secreted in a rhythmic way. This provides intervals for the mother to relax and the baby to receive oxygenated blood from the mother. When Oxytocin is induced, artificially, as induced labor, the intervals become very short thereby causing asphyxia in the baby resulting in trauma for both mother and the foetus. Induced labor is done for the convenience of adults to reduce the waiting time.

The mother's acceptance of the pregnancy and the natural process of delivery, holds key to help make the birthing process happy and comfortable.

If the mother has taken the whole pregnancy with a positive attitude, endorphins are released by the brain cells, which act as pain relievers to the mother. This establishes the mother's feeling of wellness at the same time transmitting it to the child, who gets ready for the whole new experience.

If the mother feels stressed, Cortisols and other stress hormones are released thereby affecting the foetus.

During birth, the father or whoever is assigned to accompany the mother has to be clear about the plan and try as much as possible to get that done.

- No induced labor, or epidural, it is not the length of the labor that is critical more than the safety of the labor itself. If the adults prevail on hastening the labor, they interfere with the wise, natural mechanism which is protective of the lives involved.
- Waiting for the natural process for expulsion
- The Birthing position that was arrived at - squatting position or birthing stool with all the needed apparatus for natural birth must be followed through.

- Skin-to-skin immediately after birth,
- No cutting of the umbilical cord
- Waiting for the placenta to eject on its own
- latching on to mother's breast are two important points to consider at the time of birth.
- Measuring the weight and length of the baby can wait, till the mother and baby are comfortable.

These will have to be followed, whatever the mode of birth. If there is a medical emergency for the mother, the father or the baby's sibling have to provide the skin to skin experience for the new born.

As soon as the mother is able to handle the baby, she should take over and allow the baby to latch onto the mother's breast for the first feeding.

Consciousness for all including the mother and the adults assisting, that birthing is a traumatic experience for the baby, is important, since there is a severing of the physical connection with the previous environment, inside the womb, which is practically a wound performed on the baby. So it is therefore of high priority to reduce the effect of this injury. After the child makes his journey through the vaginal passage, and arrives, his sense of physical and psychological security is the most important aspect that needs attention. The preliminary tests and APGAR tests can wait until the child gets the first comfortable skin to skin with the mother following which latching onto the breast can be expected. After this, the child can be taken for the tests if needed.

After birth:

Today, I will be talking about care of the baby, after birth. After the initial skin to skin and latching to the breast, the baby is laid to sleep on a soft bedding – preferably an old cotton sari quilt on the floor, on a straw mat.

Depending on the weather of the place, attempts to clothe the baby must be conducive to maintain average room temperature. If it is warm, it is better, to leave the child with just a thin cotton covering.

There is no need for gloves, socks, cap, full length dresses when the climate is warm. If the weather is cold, maybe a vest or a full sleeve shirt maybe needed. The hands and legs should be free for movement. Reusable cloth nappies must be handy and stored in a closed container, after use, for periodic washing.

Meconium the first sticky excreta is released within 36 hours after delivery. It is normal for it to be dark or black in colour. It may be released over a few or several days.

The skin to skin time with the mother must be continued whenever possible with the mother. The child can be lain prone on the mothers, fathers or siblings chest, consistently without changing hands frequently.

Ideally the baby is not bathed for ten days, but gentle wiping of the body can be done. Please avoid, lotions, powders creams of any sort. If the child has nails, it is ok to clip it gently, using our teeth, hygienically. Later the child's nails can be very gently cut using a small scissor, when the child is asleep.

Bathing can start from the 10th day. It is best if the mother or father give bath to the child, they can learn how to, before birth itself, and start right away. Experienced adults can just supervise. Bathing has to be an enjoyable experience for both the adult and the child. It is important to get things ready, handle the baby gently, and talk to the child during the process. The water for bathing should be lukewarm. It is good to use natural bath cleansing powders or oils - like channa dhal or moong dhal powder and warm coconut oil.

If the child seems to enjoy the bathing experience, it is good to bathe the child everyday. Hairwash can be scheduled once or twice a week.

Feeding: Breast feeding is a must and is a non negotiable for the baby. It is important for the adults around not to ever mention paucity of milk flow, so that the mother never thinks of that possibility. The baby has to make the effort to latch and suckle at the breast, without which the lactation will not be initiated. It may take upto even 1.5 minutes, for the first drop of colostrum or milk to come out, while suckling is happening. The adults must not give up and start feeding formula. Even mothers who had C section and recover from anesthesia, are capable of feeding the baby. The mothers need to trust their body completely, and rely only on themselves for providing food for the baby's survival. In rare case of low milk flow, the baby must keep suckling as slowly, milk flow will stabilize. The longer the baby suckles, the more is the milk production. The mother's body knows how much milk is needed for her babies, and produces the required amount. Rashly substituting formula, assuming that milk production is inadequate will have serious mental and physical health consequences for the baby. The child feeding on the breastmilk is important for the mother. The lactation is what helps the mother to regain her body shape, naturally besides restoring her hormones for regular menstrual cycle, that will start in a few months after delivery.

The breast must not be forced or thrust for the child to suckle. A gentle brush of the breast on the child's cheek will get the smell of food for the child to naturally latch. Without one breast emptying, the child should not be shifted to the other breast, just because the milk leaks from it copiously. The child will show signs of continuing hunger, after emptying one breast, only then the mother should shift to the next breast to continue the feed.

While feeding, focus on the baby's eyes, and when he makes eye contact, that is a conversation point. Talk to the baby – he will smile or laugh with nipple in the mouth. When we sit as a family to eat at a table, those who finish early, wait for the others to complete their dinner, which is a time for conversations. Same way the baby eagerly latches to assuage his hunger pangs first and then slowly takes time to complete the rest of his feed. Patience is needed from the mother for this process. Bottle feed does not provide for these beautiful moments, when the flow is constant and the baby has to finish the bottle at one go.

A cushion to rest the mother's arm while she continues to hold the child is desirable. Wiping cloths to clean should be kept handy. The mother would need access to drinking water while she is feeding. The child may also pass urine while feeding, hence if there is a basin to collect the urine, it will be comfortable to continue feeding.

After the feed is complete, the baby can be gently held upright to release burps. The child's stomach is in its nascent stage of digestion and hence cannot handle too much of milk at a single point in time. Hence the adults must observe the child and wait for the signals to start feeding. If the child turns away from the breast, that is a sign of satiation. No more forcing the baby to feed.

It is important for the mother to sleep next to the baby and whenever the baby sleeps. It provides the psychological security for both the mother and the baby. It is very important for the mother to spend time with the baby alone, apart from the feeding or sleeping time. Just her own time, which should be possible every day. The father's role, is mainly to limit the number of visitors coming to see the baby. He needs to be clear on this matter to friends and relatives alike. Visitors can be permitted only during the time when the mother is feeling comfortable to receive them. Preparation of the visitor, on hygiene and a soft approach towards handling the baby, is of utmost importance, even at the cost of repetition or their prior knowledge.

Home environment:

The room where the baby is, must be a slightly darkened room with a feeding chair (- the child should be able to see the mother clearly), with a place to sleep along with the mother. A small supply shelf, with wipes, water, must be available next to the feeding chair. This is the room where the mother and child spend time together, private and cozy.

Preferably visitors should not be allowed into this room. The set up for changing and bathing of the baby can be done in the same room. The movement mat for the baby can be in a common area. It is a good idea to have a large mirror for the child to see himself when movement happens. Mobiles are an opportunity for visual sense and tracking.

An adjustable mobile stand and a basic set of mobiles, like Munari, Octahedron, Gobbi, dancing figures, objects from nature. The Munari mobile is useful in the first month as it has black and white geometrical shapes. Other mobiles have a limited set of colours, and hence stimulate the growing vision and focus of the child. These can be used until the 5th month or till the child starts creeping on his own. Children when they start movement, will reach out to touch or hold the mobile.

Natural household sounds doors closing, adults and siblings talking and moving around, birds calling out, indoor or visible plants, sounds from the kitchen can all be a part of the environment. It is most important for the adults to follow a routine- bathing should always be followed by a feed. There should be a significant time gap between the previous feed and the bathing of the baby. In the morning, as soon as the child wakes up, feeding will be necessary. The time does not matter, but the order in which they happen is critical.

Be sure that there is no over stimulation in the environment, like cartoon figures and jazzy colours. The child should be talked to, while feeding, changing, bathing, at every possible opportunity, as the child would surely absorb the language, even though he may not respond.

Make sure that there is a supply table close to the changing area, to wipe the child, change cloth nappies and a storage bin for nappies waiting to be washed.

The child lies down in a supine position, when he is lying on his back, and in a prone position when he is lying on his chest.

Pictures on the walls: It is good to keep it constant for the first few months, after which if you find the child not looking at them, change them one at a time, with an interval of atleast one week in between.

It is good to lay the child on prone, starting with 10 seconds, to go on for one minute when he gains comfort of the position. Laying in prone, and supine is always done by the adult, and have the same comfort for the child. Laying on prone, gives the child a different perspective of the environment around him. He may take sometime to get used to the position, but that does not mean that he will dislike the position always.

Once the child has started flipping, it is a good idea to keep a small rattle or a small hold-able object in his eye range, on the side that he is most comfortable to flip. This maybe continued for a couple of weeks, after which the object can be placed on the other side, so that the child will try to flip over to the other side. Let the child always be the one to make an effort to flip back to the supine position, it should not be done by the adult.

If the child starts to make an effort to creep, loose fitting clothes should be avoided. Anything that restricts or stops the child's movement will restrain his effort in moving.

Toileting – need to see the body language, movement of the viscera. Start lifting the legs for passing motion from birth. Habituating a posture is necessary for a certain pattern and memory. Do not make child sit before his spine is ready – which he will show by attempting to sit up by himself. Then you can start making him sit on your legs for passing motion.

Prayer- Senses stimulation is important, which is more than possible when there is prayer time. Holding up hands, lighted lamp, chanting, and singing help a certain pattern for neural synapses.

Habit forming – toilet, feeding (more with child's expressing hunger – look out for cues) bathing (on legs). Language development- from conception on, garbled sounds start getting clearer and clearer. Gurgling sounds and salivating shows signs of talking interest. Singing, chanting, stories and speaking about what is happening to the child or around the house where they can see, is important. Preparing the child for visitors, or new environments with softly explaining to them, is vital to language development as much as stranger acclimatization. Picture stories, by adults only and not from screen or from devices, besides songs are the way to improve language. Mother tongue holds key to language development. No baby talk. Putting small objects in the mouth is a characteristic, it is important for parent to recognize this as a sensitive period of the child.

Songs:

3 months ஆழி தோழி.., தித்தித்தா ராமையா..,

4 months தப்போ தப்போ… (little help maybe needed for joining hands)

Light lamps, chant, child should see lip movement and hear the sounds of chanting.

5 months… contd.. creeping, textured, rolling articles to be shown including rattles.

7 months - அப்பம் சுட்டு.. sense of smell, stone and அப்பம் difference.

SENSITIVE PERIODS: Periods of interest spurt in learning certain skills.

How to prepare the home environment for it?

Order& Math:	0 to 5 years
Music and Language:	7 month in utero till 6 years
Small objects:	1 to 2 years

Movement:

　0 to 2.5 years – for development of movement

　2.5 to 5 – coordination of movement which includes grace and courtesy.

Refinement of senses:　　　　0 to 2.5 – exploration through senses.

　　　　　　　　　　　　　　2.5 to 4 years – refinement of senses.

　Reading:　　　　　　　　4 to 5 years

　Writing:　　　　　　　　3.5 to 4 years.

　Mathematics:　　　　　　Awareness- birth onwards

　Peaks at-　　　　　　　　4 to 6 years

　Spatial relationships:　　　From birth onwards

　　　　　　　　　　　　　　1.5 to 2 years peak of awareness.

　　　　　　　　　　　　　　2.5 to 6 years – refinement.

8.4　Home Set Up and Early Education[31]

8.4.1　Tenets of Montessori

- Mixed age classrooms.
- Uninterrupted 3 hour Work cycle.
- Simple, Elegant and Aesthetic environment.
- Child sized furniture
- Barrier free access to Materials and the guide.
- Self correcting scientifically designed materials.

8.4.2　For expecting parents

- Are you excited to see your new born baby?
- Have you thought of what form of education you want to give your Child?

---

[31] *https://cascadefls.org/pdfs/cascadefls-montessori-info-kit.pdf*

- How about an education system where you can participate in the process of educating your children?
- How about receiving year long assistance and tips on parenting?

> "Education is a natural process carried out by the human individual, and is acquired not by listening to words, but by experiences in the environment."
>
> **Maria Montessori**

In Closing

The primary goal of creating this important compilation is to educate Indian girls and boys about their rights and responsibilities in marital life, as well as to help them make informed decisions about whether marriage is right for them. While the need for comprehensive preparation that can ensure a happy married life is often mentioned by elders, only when one reaches a certain age, it emerges that these preparations should have begun much earlier. Understanding all these aspects in the book holds the key to successfully starting your own family unit.

Book Reviews

Drawing from her personal experience, Vidya Shankar Chakravarthy has compiled Sakhi, a premarital guide to relationships and parenting, as a comprehensive template for women of diverse ages, backgrounds and religious beliefs. The booklet covers all aspects of marital life as well as critical areas to look out for in case of relationship breakdown. A must read for anyone wishing to adequately inform themselves prior to entering a relationship or walking away from it.

Vasanti Sundaram, *Biographer & Actor*

The author has done a superb job. From A to Z for boys and girls from romance to divorce, abortion to adoption. A useful guide on complicated life issues. A neat work on premarital problems to post marriage baggage. Highly readable and crisp on all the topics.

Narmada Sampath, *Former Addl Advocate General*
International accredited mediator.

www.ingramcontent.com/pod-product-compliance
Lightning Source LLC
Chambersburg PA
CBHW052119030426

42335CB00025B/3059